The Automobile

DATE DUE

Demco, Inc. 38-294

The Automobile

JAMES LINCOLN COLLIER

Marshall Cavendish
Benchmark
New York

Marshall Cavendish Benchmark
99 White Plains Road
Tarrytown, NY 10591-9001
www.marshallcavendish.us

Library of Congress Cataloging-in-Publication Data

Collier, James Lincoln, 1928-
The automobile / by James Lincoln Collier.
p. cm. — (Great inventions)
Includes bibliographical references and index.
ISBN 0-7614-1877-6
1. Automobiles—Juvenile literature. I. Title. II. Series: Great
inventions (Benchmark Books (Firm))

TL146.5.C65 2005
629.222—dc22
2004022109

Series design by Sonia Chaghatzbanian

Photo research by Candlepants, Inc.

Cover photo: Randy Faris/Corbis

The photographs in this book are used by permission and through the courtesy of: *Corbis:*
Walter Smith, 2, 78; Wolfgang Kaehler, 9; Hulton-Duetsch Collection, 14, 20, 28, 31, 52;
Underwood & Underwood, 22; Bettmann, 24, 26, 29, 40,44, 47, 48-49, 50 (both), 54, 58, 60, 61, 65,
77, 80, 85; Duomo, 32-33; William Gottlieb, 63; Owen Franken, 66; Chuck Savage, 69; George
Disario, 70; Roy Morsch, 74; Eric Robert/SYGMA, 79; Tom & Dee McCarthy, 86; China Photos,
88-89. *Bridgeman Art Library:* Bibliotheque des Art Decoratifs, Paris/Archives Charmet, 8, 16;
Collection Kharbine-Tapabor Paris, 11; Private Collection/Archives Charmet, 42.
Getty Images: Hulton Archive, 13, 18, 36, 38, 72, 76; 83.

Printed in China

1 3 5 6 4 2

CONTENTS

The Automobile

THIS STRANGE-LOOKING RACE CAR WAS POWERED BY ELECTRICITY AND HELD MANY SPEED RECORDS IN THE 1890s. IT WAS BUILT AND DRIVEN BY A FRENCHMAN, CAMILLE JENATZY, AND WAS THE FIRST CAR TO REACH SPEEDS OF 100 KILOMETERS (62 MILES) PER HOUR. AT THE TIME, THE FRENCH WERE LEADERS IN BOTH CAR DEVELOPMENT AND RACING. THIS PHOTOGRAPH WAS TAKEN ABOUT 1900.

Self-Propelled Machines

Probably no invention has changed American life so dramatically and swiftly as the automobile. Without the automobile, our suburban centers—and the lifestyle that goes along with them—could not have existed as they do today. Our vacation customs and leisure habits demand cars to take us to beaches, hunting and fishing grounds, clubs, resorts, and concert halls. Today the bulk of the goods we buy so profusely are shipped by truck, not railroad. Many residents of our largest cities, such as Los Angeles, depend upon cars, not buses and trains, for transportation.

But for Americans, the car is not simply transportation. It is a symbol of status and success. Coming home with a new car is, for many, one of the most significant experiences of their lives. For young people, getting a driver's license is a rite of passage, the sign that they are independent of their families and ready for adulthood, more important to many than the right to vote or marry. American lives, to an astonishing extent, are built around automobiles. Nor is it just Americans: Europeans, Japanese, and others depend on their cars. Today major cities in developing nations, such as Jakarta in Indonesia, are clogged with automobile traffic.

A STREET IN JAKARTA, INDONESIA. TEN TO FIFTEEN YEARS AGO THIS STREET WOULD HAVE BEEN RELATIVELY EMPTY. AUTOMOBILE USE HAS BOOMED IN RECENT YEARS IN MANY DEVELOPING NATIONS. AS PEOPLE EARN MORE MONEY, THEY SPEND MUCH OF IT ON CARS.

Automobiles have brought much that is good to human life, but they come with problems as well, among them air pollution, tens of thousands of accidental injuries and deaths each year, wars over oil, and the use of resources that might be better spent in other ways. But to better understand these issues, it is important, first, to examine where cars came from.

People began dreaming of a carriage or cart that could move itself as far back as we can go in history. The first hint of a way to do it came in about 100 C.E. when a Greek philosopher, Heron of Alexander, worked out a way to use steam to revolve a ball on an axle. For some 1,600 years, that was as far as it went. Finally in 1711 an Englishman named Thomas Newcomen built the first practical steam engine. The Newcomen engine used steam to propel a piston down a hollow cylinder. This idea of using force to push a piston down a cylinder is basic to the automobile engine of today.

Newcomen, and others, were mainly interested in using the steam engine to pump water and to drive machinery in the factories that were rapidly springing up in England and elsewhere in the world as the Industrial Revolution gathered force. Machines such as cotton looms, previously run by waterpower, were switched to steam.

However, it quickly occurred to people to use steam engines to propel carts and carriages as well. Several Englishmen appear to have made great strides in developing the steam car, but the first practical one was designed by a Frenchman, Nicolas-Joseph Cugnot, who built a steam "tractor" for towing artillery. It employed two steam-driven pistons, which worked much like the legs of a bicyclist, to turn a heavy wheel.

Into the nineteenth century other Europeans built a variety of steam wagons, carriages, and buses. Some of these were quite workable, but it soon became clear that the best method of steam travel was the train. In the years following 1820, railways expanded rapidly across England, then Europe, America, and elsewhere.

But the steam engine had certain drawbacks. For one, it couldn't go anywhere until a fire had been built and a large amount of water had

STEAM CARS REMAINED A POPULAR FORM OF TRANSPORTATION WELL INTO THE TWENTIETH CENTURY. THIS FRENCH STEAM BUS DATES FROM 1872, BEFORE THE FIRST GAS-DRIVEN AUTOMOBILES WERE BUILT. STEAM ENGINES WERE POWERFUL BUT HAD SEVERAL DRAWBACKS, INCLUDING THE TIME NEEDED TO FIRE UP THE BOILER.

been set to boil. For another, it was heavy and cumbersome: a large amount of the space in a steam auto was taken up by the engine. So people began looking for other ways to drive a piston down a hollow cylinder. The answer was found in the creation of certain fluids that could be extracted from coal and oil.

In 1825 Michael Faraday, today renowned for his studies of electricity, extracted benzene from coal tar. Benzene was highly inflammable and could be made to explode easily. At around the same time, two other inflammable liquids were extracted from oil—what we today call kerosene and gasoline. Between 1856 and 1860 several European experimenters worked out the first crude internal-combustion engines. These were the prototypes of the tens of millions of engines in use today in cars, trucks, motorboats, snowmobiles, lawn mowers, and many other types of machines.

The basic principle of the internal-combustion engine is simple: an explosive fluid is introduced into a cylinder and fired. When it explodes, it drives the piston down the cylinder. The piston is attached to a rod that cranks a heavy "flywheel," and the momentum of the flywheel drives the piston back up the cylinder, pushing out the exhaust gases as it goes.

In practice there are many technical problems. For one, combustion requires oxygen, thus, the explosive fluid has to be mixed with air. For another, there needs to be some sort of device to fire the mixture. For a third, there have to be valves that open and shut to let the mixture into the cylinder and let the exhaust gas out. In addition, the cylinder has to be tightly sealed so that explosive power doesn't leak out through cracks. And everything has to be carefully timed.

Over the next few years, improvements were made to the design of this very basic engine. By the early 1860s workable internal-combustion engines, which used the sort of gas burned in the lamps of the time, were in use. Another important step forward was made in 1862 when a Frenchman, Alphonse Beau de Rochas, presented the theory of the four-stroke cycle. This notion was based on the discovery that if the mixture of air and the explosive fluid were compressed first, it would explode with greater ferocity. Rochas never built a prototype, but his idea quickly became known.

Early internal-combustion engines were adequate for running pumps and small machines, but were not really able to drive a carriage. The breakthrough that led to the self-propelled carriage was made by four Germans in the years between 1866 and 1876. The first of these was Nikolaus August Otto. In his late twenties he began hearing about internal-combustion engines and decided to build one himself, using liquid fuel such as kerosene or gasoline. For years he struggled. Then he formed a partnership with Eugen Langen, a businessman and engineer, and their new company began producing workable stationary engines.

In 1872 Gottlieb Daimler joined the Otto-Langen firm. Daimler had begun his career working for a gun maker. Later he went on to study engineering and became fascinated by the internal-combustion engine. Daimler brought Wilhelm Maybach to the firm with him as an engineering assistant.

WILHELM MAYBACH AND GOTTLIEB DAIMLER'S SON PAUL OCCUPY THE FRONT SEAT OF THE FIRST FOUR-WHEEL DAIMLER CAR, WHICH WAS REALLY A MODIFIED WAGON. THE MODERN STYLE OF AUTO BODY WAS DEVELOPED LATER.

In the early 1870s Daimler and Maybach began experimenting with the four-stroke engine envisioned by de Rochas. By 1876 they had produced a design that they patented, and two years later they had a working four-stroke engine. Meanwhile, the company had sold 2,000 of its older two-stroke stationary engines. The internal-combustion engine was no longer merely a hobby for experimenters, but a new and exciting device with limitless possibilities.

Soon, however, Otto and Daimler disagreed over various policies. In 1882 Daimler left to form his own company, taking Maybach with him. They developed a "hot tube" device for igniting the fuel, in which the tube was heated from outside the cylinder by a steady flame. When the air-and-fuel combination was compressed, some of it was driven into the tube, where it exploded, firing the gas. Soon Daimler built a bicycle driven by his four-stroke engine.

At the same time another experimenter, Carl Benz, was also building a tricycle powered by an internal-combustion engine. It used a sparking device—similar in principle to a modern spark plug—rather than a hot tube, for ignition. It could "shift gears" through a system of belts. It also included a differential, a gearing system that compensates for the fact that the left and right wheels of a vehicle move at different speeds when it is turning.

In 1885 both Benz and Daimler were testing their motor-driven vehicles in the streets. On November 10, 1885, Daimler's son Paul drove the motor bicycle a distance of about 2 miles (3.2 kilometers). Daimler continued to improve his engine. In 1887 he began to grant licenses to manufacturers in other countries to produce stationary engines for industrial use. Soon both Benz and Daimler had developed a four-wheel car powered by a two-cylinder V engine with a carburetor that worked much like later ones did.

By this time, locals had heard about the noisy new machines being tested in the workshops. A newspaper called Daimler's experimental vehicle a "repugnant, diabolical device dangerous to the life and well-being of the citizens." Attacks like these made Daimler nervous about testing his machine in public. Finally his wife, Bertha Daimler, grew annoyed by her husband's caution. One day at five in the morning, while Daimler was asleep, she awoke her older boys. The three of them started the car and set off for a drive from their home in Mannheim to Pforzheim, about 25 miles (40.3 kilometers) away. The boys had to get out and push the car up some hills, but they made the round-trip successfully.

By 1891 both Benz and Daimler were selling four-wheel motor vehicles. But it is incorrect to say that Benz and Daimler invented the automobile. Many other people had been experimenting with both the internal-combustion engine and other types of self-propelled vehicles. One of these was an eccentric genius named Siegfried Marcus. He moved restlessly from one thing to the next, dabbling in electricity, chemistry, and telegraphy. In 1865 he produced a small cart driven by a benzene engine, but he soon lost interest in cars and never followed up. In America in the mid-1830s, Alfred Drake of Philadelphia began experimenting with internal-combustion engines, and Stuart Perry of New York patented one in 1844. Ideas for the automobile came from many

The earliest Panhard-Levassor cars were based on wagon designs. But by 1896 the company had developed the forerunner to the modern automobile body, which was the basis for future models. The motor is in front under a cover. There are headlights, fenders, and a convertible top. Passengers face forward.

people. But it was Daimler and Benz who kept driving forward until they had automobiles that actually worked. They were the first to produce and sell cars on a regular basis.

The Daimler and Benz machines were essentially motorized four-wheel bicycles. It was two Frenchmen who developed the basic design for the automobile that is still used today. Daimler expected to make money not so much by building automobiles, but by granting foreigners licenses to build his engines. He contacted two French engineers named Emile Levassor and René Panhard. They admired the Daimler engine, but disliked the rest of the German's vehicle. They set about redesigning it and in 1894 produced the prototype of the modern automobile. The engine was in the front to weigh down the wheels there so they could grip the road better. They abandoned the belt system used to change speeds and introduced a clutch and a set of gears. The engine was enclosed by a hood. The body was not just a modification of a carriage or bicycle frame but was specifically designed for a car.

The Panhard-Levassor model quickly became the premier car in the world. Steered by levers or tillers rather than wheels, their engines had to be started by cranks. Still, they were surprisingly reliable, and for the moment, the French took the lead in both car manufacturing and automobile use. It was said that by 1900, France was in the midst of an automobile "frenzy."

The French had one important advantage over other nations. Almost a century earlier Emperor Napoléon Bonaparte—as well as some French kings who had ruled before him—had created a good road system for the country, to aid commerce and to make it easy to move troops swiftly from place to place. French motorists had good roads to drive on, which was not the case in many other places, including the United States. Nonetheless, other nations began operations of their own, among them England and Italy. By 1900 Europe had a small, but booming, automobile industry.

It is important to remember, however, that these early cars were very

IN THE 1890s AUTOMOBILE COMPANIES WERE SPRINGING UP ACROSS EUROPE. THIS EARLY PEUGEOT, A MAKE THAT IS STILL MANUFACTURED, USED A DAIMLER ENGINE AND HAD PASSENGERS IN THE "BACK" FACING THE DRIVER, INSTEAD OF ENJOYING THE ONCOMING VIEW. THE CAR COULD REACH SPEEDS UP TO 15 MILES (24 KILOMETERS) PER HOUR.

expensive. It was taken for granted that only the rich could afford them. The wealthy wanted showy cars with costly wood paneling, leather seats, and gleaming nickel plating. Thus, in many respects, these earlier cars were among the most spectacular ever made.

It was all new, and it was all happening in a rush. But, in fact, two other types of automobiles were competing with the gas-driven ones. For one, steam vehicles continued to be developed. These vehicles, although cumbersome, were very powerful. In 1878 one of these could run at 26 miles (41.9 kilometers) per hour carrying sixteen people. Another weighed 28 tons (25.4 metric tons) and could carry four times its weight. But many steam cars were sold for ordinary use. They continued to be popular well into the twentieth century.

There was also much interest in electric cars. Scientists had been studying electricity for more than a hundred years. Electric storage batteries, electric motors, and generators were well developed. It was simply a matter of applying electricity to a vehicle. By 1890 a number of experimental electric cars were being developed, and within a few years they were setting speed records: in an 1899 test an electric car reached 65 miles (104.7 kilometers) per hour.

Electric cars had many advantages. They were quiet; gave off no smelly fumes; were fast, reliable, and easy to start. But they had serious drawbacks as well. For one, the electric car was more expensive to build than the gas car and three times more expensive to operate. For another, it could travel only 20 to 50 miles (32.2 to 80.5 kilometers) without having to be recharged. Nonetheless, at first steam and electric cars were more popular in America than gas cars: in 1899 most of the 2,500 automobiles produced in the United States were steam or electric.

But the gas car was improving rapidly. Speed records were broken every year. Early automobiles had used hard rubber tires, like the ones used on horse-drawn carriages. The pneumatic tire, a version filled with air, had been patented in 1845 but had never been widely used. In 1888 John Boyd Dunlop developed a pneumatic tire for bicycles. Three years later two Frenchmen, the Michelin brothers, who had a business working in leather and rubber, developed a pneumatic tire for cars. These tires were easily punctured, however—roads of the time were dotted with nails lost from horseshoes. Even on a short trip, a car owner might have to repair the tires several times. In 1904 carbon black was added to rubber for additional strength and hardness. Then came tires that could be easily taken off, patched, and pumped up again.

The steering system was also significantly improved. In the earliest

JOHN BOYD DUNLOP WITH HIS PNEUMATIC-TIRED BICYCLE. SHORTLY AFTER DUNLOP'S BREAKTHROUGH, THE MICHELIN BROTHERS ADAPTED THE PNEUMATIC TIRE FOR USE ON THE AUTOMOBILE.

cars the entire axle turned on a pivot, as it did in wagons. In 1902 Sterling Elliot invented a "knuckle" that allowed the front wheels to turn while the axle remained fixed. This system made steering quicker and more precise.

By 1910 windshields were coming into use. Soon safety glass, windshield wipers, and the rearview mirror were introduced. The advantage was swinging to the gas car, and by 1910 the electric automobile had become obsolete—although it would experience a comeback almost a century later. Steam cars lasted longer, but slowly their use dwindled, too. The gas-driven auto would dominate the market for years to come.

IN THE UNITED STATES, ROADS WERE POOR, AND FOR A LONG TIME, RAILROADS WERE THE BEST MEANS OF
OVERLAND TRANSPORTATION. THIS VERY EARLY TRAIN HAD DOUBLE-DECKER CARS. PASSENGERS COULD TAKE IN
THE OPEN AIR, AS WELL AS THEIR SHARE OF SMOKE AND CINDERS. THE TRAIN'S "ATLANTIC" ENGINE HAS BEEN
PRESERVED AND IS STILL IN OPERATING CONDITION TODAY.

America Gets into the Game

During the second half of the nineteenth century, the United States was brimming with inventiveness. The electric light, the electric motor, sound recording, the telegraph, the telephone, and many other new devices were being developed there. American industry was growing at an enormous rate and soon would become the largest industrial machine in the world. It is therefore surprising that America lagged behind in the development of the automobile.

One big problem was the poor quality of American roads. By the time the first autos were being tried out, most American roads were still ruts running through woods and farmland—deep with mud in the spring and almost impassable in the northern states in winter except by sleigh. Americans had long depended on water for transport—lakes, rivers, canals, and the ocean. Later the new railroad system, developing rapidly after 1830, had become the primary means for moving people and goods from city to city.

Although a few Americans had been experimenting with the internal-combustion engine, interest in building a motorcar was slow to arise. Then, in 1876, a Centennial fair was held in Philadelphia where some crude internal-combustion engines—one built by Elwood Haynes—were exhibited. People began to see the possibilities, and by the 1880s several tinkerers, in barns and small workshops, were attempting to

AN EARLY GAS-POWERED OLDSMOBILE, ONE OF MANY INNOVATIONS TO COME.

build gas-driven automobiles. By the early 1890s several workable cars had been built, but none of them had been put into production. As a consequence, during the 1890s rich Americans began importing Panhard-Levassor cars from France—unquestionably the best vehicles available at the time.

The first real American carmakers were two brothers, Frank and Charles Duryea, working in Springfield, Massachusetts. In 1893 they produced an internal-combustion car using a one-cylinder two-stroke engine fired by an electric spark. The Duryeas actually produced eighteen cars before they fell to quarreling and ended the partnership.

The first truly successful American car was built by R. E. Olds, who gave his name to the Oldsmobile, still on the road today. Olds's father owned a gas-engine works in Lansing, Michigan. Nonetheless, Olds's first car was steam driven. In 1899, backed by a millionaire, he began producing cars. His first ones were expensive and did not sell well. He then began experimenting with cheaper models. As he was doing so, his factory caught fire. All the models were destroyed except one that happened to be near the door and was shoved into the yard ahead of the flames. Olds had no choice but to manufacture that one.

That model turned out to be the famous Curved Dash Olds, the first mass-produced American automobile. It looked something like a buggy, with bicycle wheels and a dashboard that curved inward. It sold for $650, too much for an ordinary working man, but within the reach of middle-class Americans. In 1901 Olds sold 425 of the cars, the next year 2,100, and in 1903 he sold 3,750. The Curved Dash Olds became famous. There was even a song written about it titled "In My Merry Oldsmobile." The American automobile industry was on its way.

Often new inventions struggle for acceptance. This was not the case with the automobile. During the second half of the nineteenth century, American cities—indeed cities everywhere—were growing at an astonishing rate. Transportation in the cities was mainly by horse-drawn vehicles—carts, carriages, cabs, and wagons. Inevitably, the streets were fouled by tons of horse manure and urine. Horses that died in the streets were often left there for days. Not only were the sights and smells unpleasant, but the waste from horses bred disease. It seemed to many people at the time that the automobile was the answer to the horse problem. Nobody yet understood that automobile exhaust was a far greater health concern than horse waste.

But there was more to the automobile's growing popularity than that. By 1900 the idea of the motorcar had captured the imagination of people everywhere. It seemed to be not merely a new and better means of transportation, but an invitation to adventure. Driving a car seemed exciting, almost magical. Most yearned to do it.

Given this attitude, few people thought very rationally about how this exciting new vehicle ought to be fitted into society. There was little concern about how the machine would affect road systems, cities, and the growing suburbs. It was a solution to the horse problem; that was as far as any thought was given to the social changes the automobile might bring about.

Nonetheless, despite the success of the Curved Dash Olds, the automobile was still a rich person's toy. Cars were expensive to make and expensive to maintain. By the first years of the twentieth century, there was talk of a "universal car" that would be cheap enough for everybody. But carmakers were still making big profits selling cars to the well-to-do. In fact, demand was outstripping supply: most carmakers in Europe and America could sell anything they produced.

As a consequence, some of the most famous "classic" cars from this period were the most expensive. One of these was the 1901 Mercedes, which some people consider to be the first modern car. The key figure in the creation of this renowned car was a wealthy enthusiast named Emil Jellinek. He was an official in the Austro-Hungarian empire, but he was also a Daimler salesman along the Mediterranean coast of France where many wealthy Europeans came to play.

AUTOMOBILE RACING BEGAN IN FRANCE, AND BY 1900 RACES HAD BECOME FASHIONABLE EVENTS, COVERED BY THE PRESS. THIS 1902 PHOTOGRAPH SHOWS SOME CARS BUILT BY ALEXANDRE DARRACQ, AT THE STARTING LINE, ABOUT TO SET OFF ON A RACE. AT THE TIME, DARRACQ CARS WERE AMONG THE FASTEST ON THE ROAD.

Jellinek decided he wanted to enter a Daimler in a local race for the publicity it would generate, but he knew that the Daimlers being made would not have much chance of winning. So he went to Daimler and said he would guarantee the sale of thirty-six cars if the company would make them to his specifications. The resulting car had several advanced features. Four-cylinder engines were becoming standard; the new Daimler would sport one that generated thirty-five horsepower. Water-cooling systems of the time consisted of tubes with fins on them; the new car would have the "honeycomb" radiator used today. Steering columns then were vertical; the new Daimler would have one that slanted back, as in modern cars. It also would have the H-plan gearshift still in use and an all-steel frame.

Jellinek also wanted a new name for the car. The French and the Germans had long been rivals; Jellinek worried that he might have trouble selling a car with a German name to wealthy French customers. As it happened, he had a young daughter famous for her beauty among the wealthy people of the area. As part of his deal with the Daimler company, the new car would be named for her—Mercedes.

The 1901 Mercedes won the race, as Jellinek had hoped, and became an instant success. It cost $12,000—a huge sum for the time, when an average worker made somewhere between $500 and $1,000 a year. The price insured that only the very wealthy could own a Mercedes. And this, combined with its many advanced features, made it the most admired car of its time. In 1903 an even better Mercedes was introduced. It is considered one of the greatest of all classic cars. The name *Mercedes* remains one of the most prestigious in the automobile world.

Around the same time, another car, perhaps even more admired than the Mercedes, first appeared. The story of this car begins with a man named Henry Royce, who had started out working in a railroad shop and had gone on to teach himself engineering. He eventually went into business, and by 1903 ran a company that made dynamos and electric cranes. Now wealthy, in that same year he bought a car, but he

CHARLES ROLLS WAS AN ELEGANT AND WEALTHY GENTLEMAN, WHO LOVED DANGEROUS SPORTS. HE FLEW EARLY AIRPLANES AND WAS PARTICULARLY INTERESTED IN THE NEWLY POPULAR AUTOMOBILE. THE ROLLS-ROYCE, DEVELOPED JOINTLY WITH HENRY ROYCE, REMAINS ONE OF THE MOST PRESTIGIOUS CARS IN THE WORLD.

found it noisy and uncomfortable. His engineering instincts told him he could do better, so he started his own automobile business. His first cars were reasonably good but not what he wanted.

Soon a wealthy young son of an English lord heard about Royce's car. His name was Charles Rolls. Like many of the aristocrats of Rolls's time, he was fascinated by the adventurous new devices of his day—airplanes, balloons, and of course cars, which he drove in races.

Rolls and Royce met. According to legend, Rolls told Royce, "You make the cars, I'll sell them, and we'll call it the Rolls-Royce." Their aim was to make a car as perfectly engineered as possible. At a time when it was accepted that cars had to be noisy, the Rolls-Royce would be silent, smooth, and durable. The secret would be the greatest attention to the smallest detail. The wood and metal finishes would be exquisite.

The first few models were successful. Rolls raced some of them and won at least once. But Rolls and Royce wanted to do better, so in 1907 they adopted a "one-model" policy—they would make only one type of car, but it would be the finest in the world.

And indeed, the Silver Ghost, so named because it moved quietly, was that. It was made until 1926, one of the longest runs any car has ever had. Many of them are still on the road today, some logging more than 500,000 miles (805,000 kilometers). One authority claims that the

THE FAMOUS SILVER GHOST, ONE OF THE MOST-DESIRED AND HIGHLY PRIZED OF ALL CLASSIC CARS. MANY ARE STILL ON THE ROAD TODAY. SOME HAVE TRAVELED MORE THAN 500,000 MILES (805,000 KILOMETERS).

Rolls-Royce is "perhaps the finest mechanical artifact that has ever been made." Not everyone would agree; but there is no doubt that the Rolls was—and is—a superb machine.

It is clear that even at that early date many people around the world had an attitude toward automobiles that was different from how they felt about the other useful devices in their lives, like telephones and heating systems. The interest of millions of people in automobiles was intense. Some even said that cars were becoming a "religion," especially in America. This may have been putting it too strongly, but it is certain that many people believed that their car was the most important thing they owned.

Given all of this, it is hardly surprising that people began racing their automobiles from its earliest days. In the 1890s France was still leading in automobile development, and the first automobile race was organized there in 1894. It was to be run from Paris to Rouen, a distance of 79 miles (127 kilometers). It was not a race in the true sense, since economy and ease of handling—not just who crossed the finish line first—were to be taken into account. But it was speed that interested everybody most. More than a hundred entries were submitted, including designs for vehicles supposedly powered by pendulums and gravity. Twenty-one cars, including steamers, showed up at the starting line. The fastest of them proved to be a steamer, which averaged 11.6 miles (18.7 kilometers) per hour. However, for technical reasons, the prize was shared by a Panhard-Levassor and a Peugeot, both using Daimler engines. Public interest was so great that the racing cars were accompanied by a reporter for the New York *Herald* on a bicycle. His and other newspaper stories about the race helped fuel American interest in cars.

Another race followed the next year and increasing numbers thereafter. The largest number were held in France, but other countries were catching the itch: Henry Ford, later to build the most important car ever made, won a race in 1896. Ettore Bugatti and Giovanni Agnelli, who would both found successful motorcar companies, won races in Italy in 1898. Among the most famous of these early races were ones

Although the French were pioneers in auto development and racing, other nations soon followed. The Italian Ettore Bugatti made many important cars. Here he is shown, wearing the derby, in the late 1930s. His son Jean is seated in the race car.

TODAY THE **NASCAR** CIRCUIT HAS A HUGE FOLLOWING BOTH IN THE UNITED STATES AND ABROAD. THIS PHOTOGRAPH SHOWS THE FAMED DRIVER JEFF GORDON, IN THE DUPONT CAR, AT THE HOMESTEAD-MIAMI SPEEDWAY IN 2000.

sponsored by James Gordon Bennett, son of the founder of the *Herald,* who was managing the European edition of the newspaper in Paris. The first of the Bennett races was mainly notable for the number of dogs that were killed. As they do today, dogs, maddened by the noisy charging machines, would run out into the path of the vehicles. One driver alone killed five dogs in the early stages of the race. He was, in turn, nearly killed by a dog, when a huge Saint Bernard leaped into his car and damaged the steering. "At 60 miles per hour the car jumped a ditch, circled two trees and rushed down the road in the opposite direction" before the driver could regain control.

These early motor races were clearly dangerous, not merely for drivers but for spectators, too. By the first years of the 1900s, stripped-down racers were able to go faster than 60 miles (96.6 kilometers) per hour, some reaching 90 miles (144.8 kilometers) per hour. Viewers, with little experience of anything traveling that fast on roads, tended to crowd onto the road to see the oncoming vehicle. As it approached they would jump back just enough to allow a narrow alley for the car to roar through. Scores, possibly hundreds, of spectators were killed.

But the drivers themselves were at the greatest risk. Little thought was given to their safety. To make the cars as light as possible, anything that might protect the driver was removed. In a race on Long Island, the mechanic was bounced out of the car on a rough patch of road. The driver didn't even slow down. In another American race, a Mercedes blew a tire. The rim caught in a trolley track, spinning the car around. The Mercedes flipped over, killing the mechanic aboard. In France, Marcel Renault, one of the founders of the famous company, was also killed in a racing accident.

But the danger did not stop people from racing cars, nor did it stop others from watching. From these beginnings, automobile racing has become a worldwide sport. The famous "Indy"—the Indianapolis 500—is followed around the world by millions of car-racing fans; and the NASCAR races are big-money events, especially in the American South, where some top drivers are more famous than baseball or football stars.

Automobile racing, however, has more than entertainment value: many advances in automotive technology were devised for racing cars, including four-wheel brakes, hydraulic brakes, shock absorbers, disc brakes, fuel-injection systems, and much more. When the value of these developments was proved on the racetrack, they were modified for production models and eventually became standard equipment, improving performance, safety, and durability. The automobile industry continues to invest heavily in racing, in part for publicity, but in part in an effort to improve its products.

By 1910 the automobile had come a long way in an astonishingly short amount of time. Less than twenty years after Bertha Daimler made that secretive 50-mile (80.5-kilometer) road trip in her motorized four-wheel bicycle, cars were able to reach 60 miles (96.6 kilometer) per hour, and magnificent vehicles such as the Rolls-Royce Silver Ghost and the Mercedes were selling by the thousands. But the universal car, affordable to all, still did not exist. It would soon appear and transform America.

HENRY FORD, ONE OF HISTORY'S MOST IMPORTANT CARMAKERS.

THREE

Cars for Everybody

Henry Ford was a typical American of his time. His father had emigrated from Ireland; his mother had Dutch ancestors. He was born in 1863 and grew up on a farm, as did the majority of Americans at the time. Like many Americans, he was eager to succeed. He was a tinkerer, curious about how things worked, and as a boy he constantly took clocks apart and put them together again. And like many Americans, he was always looking for ways to improve things.

His parents expected Henry to become a farmer like them, but it was machinery that interested the boy. All over America people were churning out inventions, finding new ways to do things. Immigrants pouring in from Europe, and other people moving from the farms, were flooding American cities. American life was changing. Henry Ford wanted to be part of this exciting new world.

At a young age, Henry Ford left the farm and moved to Detroit, where he got a job in a machine-tool factory. From there he went on to other jobs involving steam engines. In 1888 he married, found a small house where he could have a workshop, and began using his spare time to experiment with the internal-combustion engine. By 1896 he had developed a prototype for a car, and by 1899 he was trying to get an automobile company started. It was rough going. In order to make his name known, he built a car and challenged Alexander Winton to a race. Winton was one of the best-known American carmakers of the day. The race, to be held at Grosse Pointe, a town near Detroit, caught the interest of the local press and received a lot of publicity. Winton got off to an early lead, but after a while his engine began to smoke and his car slowed. Ford easily passed him. He covered the course at an average of 45 miles (72.5 kilometers) per hour, a relatively good time for the period.

The victory brought Ford the attention he had hoped for. He finally received enough backing to open the Ford Motor Company. For the first several years, he made some cars of the usual type that were fairly successful.

FIRST · CAR

HENRY FORD'S FIRST CAR WAS REASONABLY SUCCESSFUL. BUT LIKE MOST CARS, IT WAS TOO EXPENSIVE FOR A MAJORITY OF AMERICANS AND COULD BE BOUGHT ONLY BY THE WEALTHY. OWNING A CAR IN THE 1890s WAS A LITTLE LIKE OWNING A PRIVATE PLANE TODAY.

But Ford could see that there were only a limited number of wealthy people in America. There remained a huge, untapped market of less prosperous Americans who would buy cars if they could afford them. With this vision in mind, he set about designing the universal car—simple, sturdy, and cheap.

In 1908 he offered it to the public—the Ford Model T, the most famous car ever built. It was, says one auto historian, "the most maligned and the most praised, the most reliable and most cantankerous, the ugliest and most functional of all cars. . . ."

The Model T was filled with innovations. Not all of them were Ford's creations, but it was his particular genius to know a good idea when he saw it and to find a way to use it. Most cars at the time were made with a one-piece engine block—the main part of the motor in which the pistons and valves moved. The Model T sported a two-piece block instead on which the head, or "top," was separate and bolted on. This made the engine easier to build and simpler to service. In most other cars the driver sat on the right, even though in America the rule was to drive on the right, as it is today. Ford moved the driver over to the left side where he or she could better see oncoming traffic when passing. The car also had an innovative spring system, which allowed for sharper steering, and a simple but effective lubricating system. Made of vanadium steel, a European invention, the Model T was particularly durable.

Perhaps its best-remembered feature, though, for anyone who has driven a Model T, was the way it shifted speeds. Instead of gears, the power was transmitted to the wheels via belts, or bands, as they were generally called—one for low, one for high, and one for reverse. Step on one pedal and you were in low; release it and you were in high. A second pedal put you in reverse, and there was a third one for the brake. The result was that you could stop the car by stomping on any of the three pedals. Of course these bands wore rapidly. The band for reverse was the least used. Sometimes it was the only one in good enough condition to get a Model T up a hill, so drivers would often back up. But despite such quirks, the Model T was sturdy and reliable.

THE MODEL T WAS FIRST PUT ON THE MARKET IN 1908. IT WAS SIMPLE BUT INGENIOUSLY DESIGNED, STURDY AND CHEAP. AS IT DEVELOPED OVER TIME, AMERICANS BOUGHT IT IN THE MILLIONS. IT INTRODUCED THE MASSES TO THE THRILLS AND RESPONSIBILITIES OF CAR OWNERSHIP.

Above all, it was cheap. The first models were priced at $850, about a year's salary for a laboring man. In a few years the price had dropped to $600. Within ten years the price was $450, and in 1924 it had dropped to $290. Even at these prices the Model T was too expensive for the lowest-paid members of the workforce, but it was affordable for the American middle class and the better-paid blue-collar workers.

These low prices were made possible by Ford's adoption of mass-production techniques. A mass-production system depends on the interchangeability of parts. Before the advent of the modern factory system, most things were made one at a time. For example, a gun maker would fashion an individual trigger and stock for the particular barrel he was working on at the time. In mass production all the same parts are made exactly alike, so that you can put together any stock, trigger, and barrel from your supply to make a gun.

This system was probably first used by Eli Whitney to make guns for the U.S. government long before cars were invented. And it was already being used by other automakers: in 1908 three new Cadillacs, a new make that was having some success, were shipped to England. There they were taken apart. The parts were mixed up, and the three cars were reassembled from randomly chosen parts, resulting again in three fully functioning Cadillacs. The feat got a lot of publicity.

Henry Ford, thus, did not invent mass production, but he was imaginative in the way he applied it to car making. (Of course many of the ideas came from the engineers in his employ.) In particular, he was important in developing the assembly line, in which each worker added something to a car as it passed by him on some sort of conveyor.

A second important Ford innovation was his decision to start paying his workers $5 per day, an unheard-of wage at the time for a laborer. He had two reasons for doing so. For one, work on the assembly line was very tedious; workers were always quitting for other jobs. The high pay kept them at the Ford company. For another, Ford realized that under-paid workers could not afford to buy the very cars they were making. He hoped that his example would force wages up for all workers.

HENRY FORD DID NOT INVENT THE MASS-PRODUCTION SYSTEM, BUT HE WAS PARTICULARLY ADEPT AT EXPLOITING IT TO PRODUCE CARS THAT COULD BE SOLD AT REASONABLE PRICES. HE MADE EXTENSIVE USE OF THE ASSEMBLY LINE, SHOWN HERE, IN WHICH THE CARS MOVED PAST THE WORKERS, EACH OF WHOM PERFORMED ONE SPECIFIC TASK AS THE CAR MOVED BY.

Because of the great success of his cars, the vast wealth he was earning, and the $5-per-day wage, for a time Ford was one of the most popular people in the United States. It was believed that he could have easily won the presidency if he had chosen to run. In time though his fame went to his head, and his popularity dwindled. He phased out the Model T in 1927, as new inexpensive cars caught up to it. He replaced it with the very popular Ford Model A. Nonetheless, the Model T had been a major force in bringing the automobile age to America: by the time its run ended, 15 million had been made.

One group particularly fond of the Model Ts was farmers. In 1910 tens of millions of Americans still lived on farms. It was far easier to drive into town in a car than to harness horses to a carriage. Soon some farmers began remodeling their Model Ts to make them into trucks. When Ford discovered this, he launched his own line of trucks. He followed this with Fordson tractors. Farmers had already been using steam-driven machinery to increase efficiency; harvesters and harrows powered by internal-combustion engines only accelerated the process, eventually helping to create the giant industrial farms of today.

The car to compete most successfully with the Ford was the Chevrolet. The story of this make begins with a brash businessman named William Durant, who had made millions building carriages. By 1900 he realized that the automobile threatened to put carriage makers out of work permanently. In 1904 he assumed control of the small Buick company, which was having financial difficulties although the car itself was good.

At the time many businessmen were attempting to create monopolies. The point was that if a single company could control all, or most, of the production of a certain product or service, it could set very high prices, and people who needed that product could do nothing about it.

John D. Rockefeller in oil, Andrew Carnegie in steel, and many other people had built huge companies that gave them much power in their fields. Monopolies were contrary to the basic idea of the free enterprise system, in which open competition is supposed to keep prices low and quality high. The U.S. government tried—as it does today—to prevent monopolies from forming but did not often succeed.

"Billy" Durant decided to start an automobile monopoly, or trust. He asked Henry Ford to join him. Ford refused. In 1908, just as the first Model Ts were coming out, Durant formed a company he called General Motors. He began acquiring other automobile companies, such as Cadillac, as well as makers of auto parts and supplies, such as Champion which made spark plugs and W. F. Stewart which made coaches. Eventually Durant lost control of General Motors, but the company continued to grow, and in time its leading vehicle was the Chevrolet. By

"BILLY" DURANT'S ATTEMPT TO CREATE A MONOPOLY, WHICH WOULD BE ILLEGAL TODAY, LED TO THE CREATION OF GENERAL MOTORS. HE IS SHOWN HERE IN 1922 WITH THE DURANT STAR, AFTER HE HAD LEFT GENERAL MOTORS AND FORMED ANOTHER COMPANY.

the 1920s Ford and General Motors had come to dominate the American automobile business, with Ford and Chevy constantly competing to see which could outsell the other.

There were, of course, other car makers, including Chrysler, Dodge (absorbed by Chrysler in 1928), Studebaker, Hudson, Maxwell, Oldsmobile, Packard, Locomobile, Pierce-Arrow, and more. But by 1914 the nature of the American automobile business was changing. In the years after 1900 there had been some 500 people in little factories making— or trying to make—cars. By 1915 there were 170 automobile makers, and the ten largest companies were building 80 percent of American cars. Efficient mass production required huge factories and a large workforce. This in turn called for vast amounts of capital. Bit by bit the small carmakers were forced out of business or swallowed up by the larger ones.

At the same time, the American automobile industry was shooting ahead of the European. The key factor was the vast differences in the distribution of wealth. In Europe there was a tiny class of ultra-rich, a relatively small group of well-to-do middle-class people, and a huge mass of peasant farmers and laborers who could not consider buying a car. In Europe, then, the market demanded only small numbers of fairly high-priced cars.

In America the situation was different. The country had plenty of poor people working in mines, living in big-city slums, or struggling to make a go of it on worn-out farms. But there was a large, affluent middle class composed of several million families. There was also a sizable body of well-paid workers with special skills, like printers and engravers, tool-and-die makers, and many more. By 1914, when World War I began, the market for automobiles in America ran into the millions. While there would always be a demand for luxury cars, most of the business would be, as it is today, in inexpensive cars for middle-class people.

World War I helped to advance the efficiency of the internal-combustion engine. The generals quickly realized the advantage of motorized

WORLD WAR I SAW, FIRST, THE USE OF THE AIRPLANE AS A WEAPON OF WAR AND THEN, IN ITS LATER STAGES, THE INTRODUCTION OF THE HEAVILY ARMORED TANK. BOTH INVENTIONS SPURRED THE FURTHER DEVELOPMENT OF THE INTERNAL-COMBUSTION ENGINE. IN THIS PHOTOGRAPH, A TANK FROM THE WAR IS SHOWN WITH CAPTAIN DWIGHT EISENHOWER, LATER TO BE ELECTED PRESIDENT OF THE UNITED STATES, STANDING BESIDE IT.

vehicles over horse-drawn ones to carry troops, transport supplies, and haul artillery. The airplane had been developed enough to be useful in war. Planes needed more powerful engines than cars, and airplane engineers helped to improve engine technology. In the last year of the war, the tank, a moving steel fortress driven by a gas engine, proved to be a decisive weapon. Moreover, during the war, millions of soldiers became acquainted with cars and trucks and learned to drive and service them. By the end of the war, the horse-drawn wagon and the cavalry charge were finished.

The Model T and other inexpensive cars revolutionized American society, but the cars best-remembered today by classic-car fanciers are the luxury models. Unquestionably the most successful of these was the Cadillac. Most significantly, in 1912 Cadillac introduced the self-starter. Previously all cars had to be hand cranked to start the engine. Women, it was believed, were too fragile to crank a car. With the self-starter, women could not only drive without the help of a male, but could own cars. The potential driving population of the country instantly doubled, and within two years nearly all new cars had self-starters.

Today the 1914 Cadillac V-8 is considered one of the great classic cars. But perhaps the most widely admired American cars at the time were two others, the Stutz Bearcat and the Duesenberg. The Stutz Bearcat had a four-cylinder engine, at a time when most expensive cars were outfitted with six or eight cylinders. Al-

ALTHOUGH THE TERM SPORTS CAR HAD NOT YET BEEN COINED, SUCH CARS DID EXIST. ONE OF THE MOST FAMOUS WAS THE STUTZ BEARCAT, WHICH WAS FAST FOR ITS TIME. THIS VERSION OF THE STUTZ BEARCAT DATES TO ABOUT 1910.

though it weighed 2 tons (1.8 metric tons), the 1914 model could travel at 80 miles (128.8 kilometers) per hour. It was a jaunty two-seater, in every sense a *sports car* before the term had been invented. It particularly appealed to people who liked to race and so was obviously not intended for ordinary family driving.

The Duesenberg was even more famous. To this day we sometimes say, "It's a doozy" when we talk about something especially admirable. The car was spectacular in every way—made of the finest materials and engineered to perfection. It had a huge eight-cylinder engine which could generate 265 horsepower. It also featured hydraulic brakes, rare at the time, warning lights when it was time for an oil change, a stopwatch, and an altimeter on the dashboard. The Duesenberg had a top speed of 116 miles (186.8 kilometers) per hour and would do 90 miles (144.9 kilometers) per hour in second gear. The 1932 SJ supercharged model was even more powerful: it could go 130 miles (209.3 kilometers) per hour and accelerate from 0 to 100 miles (161 kilometers) per hour in 17 seconds.

Owners of Duesenbergs had the bodies customized to fit their wishes, including gold-and-ivory trim, rare woods, and thick upholstery. The finished cars cost anywhere from $15,000 to $25,000, depend-

PERHAPS THE MOST FAMOUS OF THE EARLY GLAMOUR CARS WAS THE EXPENSIVE AND ELEGANT DUESENBERG.
IT WAS POWERFUL AND COULD TRAVEL AT HIGH SPEEDS. THIS 1915 VERSION WAS CAPABLE OF REACHING
MORE THAN 100 MILES (161 KILOMETERS) PER HOUR.

THE INVENTION OF THE SELF-STARTER WAS POPULARLY BELIEVED TO HAVE OPENED THE DOOR TO WOMEN DRIVERS. WHATEVER THE CASE, MORE AND MORE WOMEN BEGAN DRIVING THROUGHOUT THE SECOND DECADE OF THE TWENTIETH CENTURY. BY THE 1920S, WHEN THE FEMINIST MOVEMENT WAS GAINING GROUND, WOMEN DRIVERS WERE TAKEN FOR GRANTED. AT THE TOP, MAUDE ODELL, ONE OF THE FIRST FEMALE TAXI-CAB DRIVERS, IN 1923. AT THE BOTTOM, A WELL-DRESSED CELEBRITY IS PICTURED IN AN EXPENSIVE CAR IN 1917.

ing on the body, more money than some people of the time could make in a lifetime. It was distinctly a car for the wealthiest people and was prized for its durability. Of the approximately 550 J and SJ models made, perhaps 200 are still being driven.

Immediately after the end of World War I in 1918, the nation experienced a financial downturn. Then came what appeared to be the roaring prosperity of the 1920s—the so-called Jazz Age. Money seemed to be everywhere, but in truth the prosperity would prove hollow. Still, people could afford to buy cars—and everybody wanted one. In addition, there was an adventurous spirit in the air: Americans were ready for anything new. Finally, there was a strong feminist movement—women had been granted the right to vote in 1920. Young women also felt that they had a right to drive cars.

Critically important at the time, the price of closed-body cars was coming down. The closed 1922 Essex Coach cost only $200 more than standard open cars. Other manufacturers were forced to follow suit. "Essex changed the entire market," one historian says. The closed car made it possible for people to drive in rain and snow. You could then count on driving your car to work every day, no matter what the weather. It was a change of vast importance. In 1920, 17 percent of the cars sold were closed; in 1927 it was 85 percent. By that year Americans owned 80 percent of the world's cars. In the United States, there were 5.3 people for every car; in France and England there were more than 44 people per car.

Yet another factor in fueling the auto craze was installment buying. Before then, Americans had paid cash for nearly everything except their homes. For most Americans the automobile was the second-most expensive purchase they ever made; and for the millions living in rented houses or apartments, the car was their biggest expense. By 1920 half of all cars were bought with loans or on time. It was the desire for automobiles that began the movement for buying on credit that is so widely accepted by Americans today.

In 1927 there came another innovation. The head of General Motors happened to see some cars that had been customized for Hollywood

By the 1920s, increased automobile use was creating a public outcry for better roads. Here workers upgrade a city street.

stars by Harley Earl. He hired Earl to start an Art and Color Section for General Motors. As it happened, new metal-stamping processes allowed for a greater variety of shapes in parts like doors, hoods, and trunk hatches. Earl and others began designing cars with shapes they thought looked "elegant" or "sassy." It was then left to the engineers to figure out how to build cars in those shapes. Some car historians have complained that the stylists took away some of the character and individuality of cars, but the public clearly liked the new looks.

As millions of Americans began driving for pleasure and business, the pressure on governments to improve the quality of poor American roads increased. A Federal Road Act in 1916 allotted $75 million for road building. In 1921 the Federal Highway Act poured more money into road construction. By 1924 the United States had 31,000 miles (49,910 kilometers) of paved roads. In 1925 the state highway numbering system was established. Road improvement became a major priority—and expense—for states, towns, and counties, as it is today. Some people objected: if the train, trolley, and subway industries had to build their own "roads," why should roads for automobiles be paid for by the taxpayers? In response, car-registration fees and other car-related taxes were allocated for road building. However, in 1929 governments spent $2.2 billion on roads and collected only about a third of it in motor-vehicle taxes. Mainly, roads were built with the taxpayers' money.

In the 1920s, then, automobile driving became safer and more convenient. It was no longer an adventure, but a routine part of American life. The effect on American culture was enormous.

The American suburbs were a product of the transportation revolution. But they did not begin with cars. By the late 1800s the cities were exploding. They were also becoming dirtier and more dangerous. To many people, cities were seen as breeding grounds for crime and disease. Those who could afford it began to look for places to live where there were quiet streets, green grass for children to play on, clean air, and birds singing.

But most jobs were in cities. Therefore the movement outward first spread along rail and trolley-car lines. In these rapidly developing outlying

THE BOOM IN SUBURBAN GROWTH IN THE 1920S AND 1930S WAS MADE POSSIBLE BY THE AUTOMOBILE.
IN THIS PHOTOGRAPH FROM 1936, A HUSBAND AND FATHER SETS OFF FOR WORK IN A LINCOLN ZEPHYR,
AS HIS WIFE AND DAUGHTER SEE HIM OFF FROM THE PORCH OF THEIR MODERN HOUSE.

areas, the middle class built large, pleasant houses surrounded by lawns within easy walking distance of railroad stations. Father walked to the station every morning to commute to his job in the city, while mother stayed home to care for the children, often with the help of a servant or two.

Since these early commuters were tied to the railroad and trolley lines, there were limits to how much the suburbs could grow. With the coming of the automobile, there were no limits. Suburbs could spread to wherever there were roads—and if there were no roads, new ones could be built. Wives could drive their husbands to the station each morning or husbands could drive themselves into the city.

The growth of the suburbs during the 1920s was phenomenal. Grosse Pointe, outside of Detroit, grew more than seven times in size during the decade. In the same period Shaker Heights, outside of Cleveland, grew tenfold; Beverly Hills, in suburban Los Angeles, grew more than twentyfold. The same was true of thousands of suburban towns across the country. One historian has said, "The decade from 1920 to 1930 saw the complete emergence of the modern residential suburb." It was the reliable, inexpensive enclosed car that made it all possible.

These new suburbanites were mostly well-to-do middle-class people—professionals or managers of the mighty American industrial machine. Working people still could not afford to own new cars, although they were increasingly able to buy used cars. But most working people, aside from farmers, lived in cities and did not really need cars. Even as late as 1945, 40 percent of American families did not own cars, and only the rich owned more than one. Nonetheless, by 1930 the middle class took car ownership for granted. Of course you had a car; and as your income improved, you naturally bought grander and more expensive ones.

The move to the suburbs was slowed by the Great Depression, which began in 1930 and ended with America's entrance into World War II in 1941. But suburban growth was not stopped, and with the end of the war it surged again.

Suburban life was built around cars. Some suburbs, especially those on the borders of cities, had bus and trolley lines that serviced the area, but most did not. Children went to school on buses, food was delivered by trucks, and getting to almost every kind of activity outside the home required a car trip. The effects were many, the most significant of which was the dispersal of the family. On farms, families worked together, played together, and ate together: most family members saw each other for hours every day. In cities, fathers, and sometimes mothers, left home for work. Most other activities took place in a neighborhood of a few square blocks. Your friends were your neighbors. Everybody shopped at the same neighborhood stores, went to the same theaters and taverns. Neighbors looked after each other's children and helped out when somebody was sick.

In the suburbs, cars allowed schools, shops, theaters, clubs, town halls, doctors' and dentists' offices, and everything else to be spread over an area of three, four, five, or more square miles. Fathers left home for work early in the morning, returned in the evening, and missed out on most of the daily activities of their families. Children left for school after breakfast; might go directly from school to play sports, meet with clubs, or just hang out with friends; and so might also be out of contact with parents, brothers, and sisters for the bulk of the day. Wives spent much time in their cars going to shops, driving their children one place or another, taking their husbands to and from the railroad station, visiting friends, and doing volunteer work. The old notion of a tightly knit community built around families had begun to change.

With people spread out over larger distances, human activities became more formalized. In the big cities there were usually enough kids of about the same age living within a couple of blocks to get up baseball, football, and other games; in suburbs children increasingly had to be driven to a field to play in an organized league. In the big cities, neighbors easily congregated around stoops, in cafés, or on sidewalks to gossip, play cards, make music, and eat and drink. In the suburbs people more often met at formal dinner parties, card parties, and in today's playdates and sleepovers, mostly arriving by car.

The automobile changed American life in some obvious ways: people were able to do things that their grandparents could never have considered, like traveling long distances to beaches, ski resorts, and hunting grounds. They could take jobs 50 miles (80.5 kilometers) from home or visit relatives across the state. But the car changed life in subtle ways Americans had not even begun to imagine.

BY THE LATE 1930S, AUTOMOBILES HAD REACHED MATURITY. THEY COULD BE DRIVEN SAFELY AND COMFORTABLY IN ANY WEATHER, WERE RELIABLE, AND WERE PRICED SO THAT MOST MIDDLE-CLASS FAMILIES COULD AFFORD ONE. HERE, A CHRYSLER IS ON DISPLAY AT AN AUTO SHOW IN NEW YORK CITY IN 1937.

The Car Comes of Age

Through the 1930s the automobile industry made steady progress in producing cars that were ever safer, more efficient, more comfortable, and easier to drive. Lights, brakes, and tires were all improved step-by-step. The curved windshield was pioneered in the 1930s and became widely used in the 1940s. Safety features were added—padding on front-seat backs in 1932, recessed instrument controls and self-canceling directional signals in 1937, sealed-beam headlights in 1939. Heaters became standard in the late 1930s. The radio was introduced as an option in 1929—but in the backseat only, so as not to distract the driver. Adjustable seats and front quarter-windows were introduced in the 1930s. The automatic transmission debuted in the late 1930s and enjoyed wider acceptance in the 1940s.

By 1940 the automobile had become the creature we are familiar with today. One authority says, "Even today, the autos of this period could be driven comfortably and dependably from coast to coast at conventional speeds on today's interstate systems." By that decade, there were people in their forties who could not remember a time when there were no cars.

Then suddenly it all came to a halt. World War II began in Europe in 1939, and in 1941 the United States joined the conflict. The car industry stopped making automobiles in order to build army vehicles, like jeeps and tanks, airplanes, and other war materials. Rubber, steel, and

DURING WORLD WAR II, AUTOMOBILE FACTORIES TURNED TO PRODUCING TANKS, AIRPLANES, AND OTHER WAR-RELATED ITEMS. WOMEN TOOK UP POSTS AT DEFENSE PLANTS TO REPLACE MEN WHO HAD GONE OFF TO THE BATTLEFIELDS. HERE, WORKERS ASSEMBLE AN AIRPLANE WING.

gasoline were needed for the war. Civilians found tires hard to get. Gasoline was rationed: an ordinary driver was allowed only about 3 gallons (11.4 liters) per week unless he or she needed more to commute to work. During the war years, few new cars were built.

When the war ended, Americans wanted all the things denied them during the war. In particular, they wanted new cars. The wave of spending on cars and household items, like refrigerators and furniture, helped to bring a long period of prosperity to the United States— the greatest ever seen until that time. Nearly everybody who wanted a job could get one. Salaries rose. People who could remember nothing but fifteen years of depression and war were now able to own things they had only dreamed of ten years before.

One result of this prosperity was a second burst of suburb building, helped by cheap mortgages guaranteed by the U.S. government to veterans of the war. This time it was not just the middle class that was moving to the suburbs, but people who had grown up in cramped city apartments or on small farms. In 1944 about 100,000 new houses were built in the United States; in 1950 the number rose to more than a million. By 1960 a third of Americans lived in suburbs.

A new federal-government program to build additional highways encouraged car use even more. The president, Dwight Eisenhower, had been supreme commander of the Allied armies in Europe during World War II. He had a general's concern for defense and was persuaded that a

Before World War II, very few four-lane highways and parkways had been built. After the war, the U.S. government instituted an extensive building program, which began the network of superhighways now crisscrossing the country. The Kansas Turnpike was built to the state line, the edge of a farmer's wheat field, where it stopped until more money was allocated to begin the Oklahoma Turnpike, which would stretch beyond.

system of superhighways would be useful in moving American troops and equipment around the country in case of war. In 1956 the Federal Highway Act awarded states 90 percent of the cost of building super-highways. Eventually $25 billion was spent on 41,000 miles (66,010 kilometers) of road. It "ushered in our modern, high-speed but safe road system." Much of the inter-city highway system that drivers use today was started by this program.

With the new prosperity, Americans no longer felt that they always had to look around for the cheapest car. They were growing used to buying on time; as long as they could make the payments, they could reach for a more impressive car.

The automobile industry was glad to oblige its customers: bigger cars are more profitable than smaller ones. From 1949 to 1959, cars in every price range grew bigger. They were, says one authority, "overpowered, undertired, underbraked," for their weight. But it was not just size. During this time, "styling was king." Cars sprouted purely decorative tail fins; chrome was stuck on wherever a place could be found for it. The 1948 Cadillac was inspired by the P-38 fighter plane. These extravagant cars were gas-guzzlers: in 1949 a large Cadillac could get 20 miles (32.2 kilometers) per gallon; by 1973 ordinary passenger cars were averaging 13.5 miles (21.7 kilometers) per gallon.

Americans didn't care: in the United States gas was cheap. Elsewhere it was not: in Europe it was two or three times the American price. Today gasoline costs about $5 per gallon in Europe. Europeans were also faced with the fact that their automobile industry had been almost destroyed by World War II. During the 1950s, carmakers in England, France, Italy, Germany, and elsewhere were struggling to get back on their feet. Japan, Russia, and China were only beginning to develop their automobile industries, and few other countries in the world had any carmakers at all and so had to depend on imports. In the postwar era 80 percent of all the world's cars were manufactured in the United States. The car culture was still an American phenomenon.

THE GREAT PROSPERITY OF THE POSTWAR PERIOD ALLOWED MANY PEOPLE, WHO WOULD HAVE BEEN UNABLE TO OWN CARS A FEW YEARS EARLIER, TO PURCHASE AN AUTOMOBILE. HERE A FAMILY ENJOYS ITS NEW PURCHASE. THE TWO-CAR GARAGE SHOWN HERE SUGGESTS THAT BY 1952, THE YEAR THE PHOTOGRAPH WAS TAKEN, THE OWNERSHIP OF MORE THAN ONE CAR WAS BECOMING COMMON.

The 1950s saw the rise of the two-car family. Previously, only the wealthy could consider owning more than one car. Suburban families had to plan who was to use the car at what times. In 1950 Ford began promoting the idea of the two-car family, still a startling idea when many urban families owned no cars at all. But more and more suburban families began buying second cars, frequently used ones, for Dad to take to work. Inevitably, the number of cars on the road jumped, from 25 million in 1945 to 61 million in 1955.

Increasingly, these cars were station wagons. They were essentially vehicles built with a third seat in the rear where the trunk would have been. Usually these rear seats could be removed or folded down to make a large carrying space. Cars that could seat six or eight passengers were being made in the early days of the industry, but the station wagon, with a wooden body which could comfortably seat six or more, became popular only in the 1930s. At first bought mainly by wealthy

THE STATION WAGON WAS INVENTED IN THE 1920S, WAS NOT WIDELY USED UNTIL THE LATE 1930S, AND FIRST ENJOYED WIDESPREAD POPULARITY ONLY AFTER WORLD WAR II. SUBURBANITES FOUND THEM USEFUL FOR TRANSPORTING CHILDREN AND CARRYING BAGS OF GROCERIES HOME. AS IN THIS PICTURE, THEY WERE ALSO POPULAR FOR CAMPING TRIPS, AS THEY HAD ROOM FOR PLENTY OF EQUIPMENT.

people, station wagons were used at summer homes to pick up luggage-laden guests at railroad stations or to take people to the beach. They were sometimes called beach wagons.

In the postwar period the station wagon was seized upon by suburban families who often found themselves carting several children to and from Little League games and band practices, along with bags of groceries and the family dog. By the end of the twentieth century, station wagons were largely pushed aside by SUVs, but used ones were still much in demand. The old pre-war "woodies," or wood-paneled models, are now admired by collectors, who lovingly restore them.

Through the 1960s the trend was for so-called muscle cars—high-performance cars with powerful engines and rapid acceleration. But already a countertrend had set in. For one, many Americans were getting tired of the large, glitzy cars the manufacturers were turning out: to many, they seemed vulgar and wasteful. For another, some people were growing concerned about the amount of gasoline these cars used. Partly they were troubled by the increased air pollution these cars caused; partly they wanted to save money. This last issue became particularly important after 1973, when, for a variety of reasons, gasoline prices shot up, and there were shortages of gas in the United States.

Gradually, Americans began to look for smaller cars. However, in the late 1950s and the 1960s, Detroit was content to turn out the big gas-guzzlers. The situation was different in Europe. Because of the high price of gas there, the narrow streets of ancient cities like Rome and Paris, and the lower incomes of Europeans, people wanted smaller cars. In the postwar period, there were far fewer affluent people in Europe than there had been. European carmakers were forced to concentrate

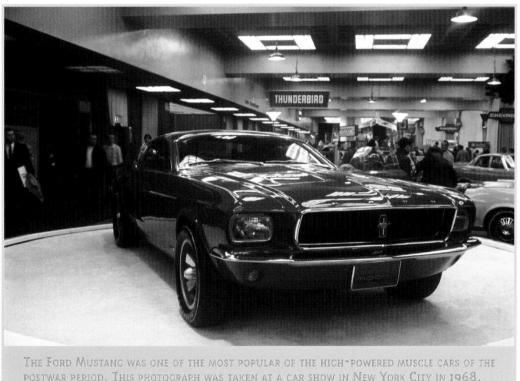

THE FORD MUSTANG WAS ONE OF THE MOST POPULAR OF THE HIGH-POWERED MUSCLE CARS OF THE POSTWAR PERIOD. THIS PHOTOGRAPH WAS TAKEN AT A CAR SHOW IN NEW YORK CITY IN 1968.

THE TREND TOWARD SMALLER CARS WITH HIGHER FUEL EFFICIENCY WAS ACCELERATED IN THE EARLY 1970S WHEN GAS SHORTAGES FORCED AMERICANS TO ENTERTAIN THE NOTION OF GREATER FUEL ECONOMY. IN 1974, WHEN THIS PHOTOGRAPH WAS TAKEN, GAS PRICES WERE SKYROCKETING.

on low-priced, fuel-efficient cars like the popular models of the Italian Fiat and the French Renault. By the 1960s European carmakers realized that they might have a potential market in the United States.

First to make headway was the famous Volkswagen Beetle. The Volkswagen was the dream of the German dictator Adolf Hitler who wanted a cheap car for his people. Because of World War II, the car never made it into production. After the war the victorious Allies set about rebuilding European industry to make the continent self-supporting as quickly as possible. With English and American help, the Volkswagen Beetle was put into production. It was small and used magnesium to reduce its weight and increase fuel efficiency. The four-cylinder engine was air cooled and set over the rear wheels, where the weight would help traction in rain and snow and shorten the drive train. The trunk was in the front. It was a cheap, simple car and Americans, especially young people, took to it in droves. In 1968, 500,000 Volkswagens were sold; by 1970 there were 4 million of them.

Through the 1960s Americans increasingly turned away from Detroit's gas-guzzlers. Foreign carmakers, observing the rocketing sales of Volkswagens, were quick to leap in. The most successful were the Japanese, who began importing cars with names strange to Americans, like Toyota, Mitsubishi, Nissan, and Subaru. In 1963 these small foreign cars made up 5 percent of all car sales in the United States. By 1971 it was 16 percent, and the figure kept rising.

American companies were slow to respond. They had commanded the market for so long, they could not believe anyone else could beat them. But with the gas shortages and the jump in gas prices of the 1970s, Detroit, the focal point of the industry, finally took notice. Carmakers introduced small fuel-efficient cars like the Ford Pinto and went on to produce various additional types of compacts and subcompacts. Nonetheless, a group of automobile journalists recently voted the Volkswagen "the car of the century."

Although the Beetle and similar cars were the most significant imports, the first small European models were another breed of automobile altogether, the sports car. The term is a loose one, but it basically means a car that is driven more for fun than for transportation. Sports cars are not meant to carry a lot of people; some are two-seaters. They usually have manual transmissions because part of the fun of driving them is the dexterous shifting involved.

Although the term was not used then, there were sports cars in the early days. The Stutz Bearcat and the Mercer Raceabout were sports cars, but the real home of the sports car was Europe, and especially England. European manufacturers produced a long line of sport models including Bugatti, Aston Martin, Riley, and Invicta.

For Americans, the most important sports car was the MG, named for Morris Garages, which first developed the model. The MG Midget appeared in 1929 and quickly became one of the most popular sports cars. It was not well known in the United States until after World War II, when the MG TC was imported. One car historian says that it "had more to do with spreading the cult of the sports car than any other machine ever built." It was relatively inexpensive for a sports car, and Americans bought a lot of them. They then often went on to purchase other, more expensive machines, notably the Jaguar, Triumph, Porsche, Ferrari, and other European makes. Eventually Chevrolet produced an American-made sports car, the Corvette, which became popular.

The American cars built from 1970 to 1985 have not been of much interest to either automobile historians or car enthusiasts. One historian wrote that "they seemed to be (and were) bolted together with a lack of overall design cohesion." It is probably unfair to dismiss all of these cars in so cavalier a fashion, but there is some truth to the statement. The cars of this period were good transportation, but have not inspired the kind of enthusiasm that early classic cars have.

The next major trend in car design came with the sudden burst of prosperity of the 1990s. Like the prosperity of the 1920s, the 1990s

SUVS AND PICKUP TRUCKS OFFERED A LOT OF ROOM FOR PEOPLE AND EQUIPMENT. BY THE 1990S
THESE TYPES OF VEHICLES WERE GROWING IN POPULARITY, DESPITE THEIR POOR FUEL EFFICIENCY.

boom proved to be hollow. But during that decade there seemed to be
plenty of money around, and Americans chose to spend a lot of it on
what came to be known as SUVs—sport-utility vehicles. These big
heavy cars with backseats that could be folded down provided a lot of
carrying room in the manner of the old station wagons.

The desire for SUVs and the craze for pickup trucks that followed had
more to do with emotion than reason, as has often been the case with car
fashions. The SUV had certain advantages. It offered a lot of room for families, luggage, and anything else. The disadvantages were the high price and
the amount of gas SUVs burned. But as long as prosperity lasted, people
were willing to pay the high sticker price and the cost of gas.

The real appeals of the SUV were its size and its power. It seemed to
be a sort of military machine in which the owner could take on the

UNQUESTIONABLY, THE BIGGER CARS OF TODAY ARE USEFUL FOR CARRYING A LOAD OF SHOPPING BAGS OR FOR HAULING FURNITURE OR HOUSEHOLD GOODS. BUT, FOR THE MOST PART, THEY ARE USED JUST AS SMALLER CARS WERE USED IN THE PAST—FOR BASIC TRANSPORTATION.

world. Of course many people had perfectly good reasons for buying SUVs, especially those who lived in mountainous country or places where there were hard winters. But SUVs had far more weight and power than most suburban families would ever need.

The vogue for pickup trucks seems to have been driven by similar emotions. A truck, of course, is useful for people who frequently buy large items such as antique furniture or bring shrubs and fertilizer home from the garden center. But most families rarely need that much carrying capacity; pickups are mainly and have always been used as cars to tote the family around and to bring home groceries from the supermarket. Pickup trucks seem to suggest a kind of do-it-yourself toughness—that the driver is a person who can cope with hard times.

Fashions in automobiles, thus, have come and gone, but there is no doubt that few Americans can imagine life without cars. In the 1920s the majority of American families did not own cars. By the end of World War II, 40 percent of them still had no cars. At that time it was rare for a family to have two cars and even rarer for high school or college students to have them. By the 1960s the number of two-car families was growing. Today the multicar family is the norm. It is taken for granted that each adult will have his or her own car. Increasingly, teenagers expect to have cars of their own as soon as they get drivers' licenses. Today there are more cars in America than licensed drivers. Thirty percent of households have three cars, and the four-car family is not rare. The car is now as central to American life as is a place to live.

PEOPLE THE WORLD OVER HAVE LONG HAD A LOVE AFFAIR WITH THEIR CARS. FOR MANY, AUTOMOBILES ACHIEVE A CERTAIN MYSTIQUE, AND THEY ARE TREATED AS OBJECTS OF GREAT BEAUTY AND VALUE.

Auto Problems

The automobile has brought much good to human beings. It has permitted people to adopt a suburban way of life where they can own large, comfortable houses and spacious yards for barbecues and jungle gyms. It has allowed them to frequently visit friends and relatives who live a hundred or more miles away, something earlier generations could not do. Cars have made it possible for people to easily get to ski resorts, beaches, and national parks for weekends and vacations. More generally, it has given people a sense of independence, a feeling that they are not trapped in their neighborhoods, but can hop in the car to join activities taking place at distant locations. The car has contributed much happiness to human life.

But, as is usually the case with technological advancement, there are drawbacks and in the case of the car severe ones. Among the first people to suffer from the arrival of the automobile was a New Yorker. On September 13, 1899, a man named Arthur Smith was driving an electric car along a city street. Ahead of him a trolley car stopped. Smith swerved to pass the trolley on the right. As he did so, a man named H. H. Bliss stepped off the trolley. Smith hit Bliss with his car and killed him instantly.

Bliss was only the first of millions to die in automobile accidents. In recent years, more than 40,000 people were killed annually by cars,

STUDIES HAVE SHOWN THAT PEOPLE USING CELL PHONES ARE FREQUENTLY DISTRACTED AND ARE MORE LIKELY TO GET INTO ACCIDENTS THAN WHEN THEY ARE CONCENTRATING EXCLUSIVELY ON THEIR DRIVING.

and at least another 3 million were injured—in the United States alone. To put that in perspective, every year thirteen times more people die in car crashes than died in the World Trade Center disaster.

In the hands of careful drivers, the automobile is perfectly safe. Accidents are rarely caused by problems with the cars, like brake or steering-mechanism failures. They are almost always caused by carelessness or plain stupidity on the part of the driver: driving too fast for the road; driving under the influence of alcohol and drugs; or inattentiveness caused by chatting, changing CDs or cassettes, or using cell phones.

When the automobile first appeared, manufacturers assumed that safety was the responsibility of the driver. Little or nothing was done to safeguard passengers or pedestrians. Unhappily, many drivers were rich young "playboys" entranced by the new machines, who wanted to drive fast and take risks. Many died in car crashes, often taking innocent bystanders with them: in 1902 a car going 20 miles (32.2 kilometers) an hour needed 59 feet (18 meters) in which to stop.

Reckless drivers caused an outcry against the car, and authorities, especially in cities, attempted to control them. In 1911 Detroit became the first city to paint lines down the centers of streets to create defined driving lanes. Cleveland had the first traffic light in 1914, and around 1919 a Detroit policeman named William Potts devised the four-way red-yellow-and-green stoplight used today. Speed limits were also posted and minimum-age requirements established for young drivers eagerly seeking their licenses.

Carmakers, too, made some effort to produce safer cars. In 1912 a racing driver, to save weight, eliminated the mechanic who usually traveled in race cars. In order to compensate for the loss of a second pair of eyes, he installed the first rearview mirror. The idea quickly caught on. The introduction of the all-steel body also reduced driver risk: wooden bodies simply exploded in crashes. Later, safety glass was introduced. In 1923 the automatic windshield wiper was coming into use, in 1928 the defroster. In 1933 the high school at State College, Pennsylvania, introduced the first driver-education program.

STUDENTS IN MODEL CARS PRACTICE THEIR DRIVING TECHNIQUE IN AN EARLY DRIVERS' EDUCATION CLASS.

In the postwar period, crash dummies were invented and a lot of crash testing began. It was becoming clear that the greatest cause of death in an accident was ejection from the car. This knowledge led to the testing of the seat belt, and in 1949 Nash installed seat belts in some of its cars. Studies at Cornell University showed that without a doubt the seat belt saved lives.

Unfortunately, most people chose not to use them even when they were available. Of the 48,000 people who bought the Nash car with seat belts, only 1,000 bothered to use them. A few years later Ford made a similar discovery. In 1956 it produced a car that included a great many safety features. That year General Motors cars outsold Ford. The industry concluded that "safety doesn't sell."

In a certain way the automobile industry could not be blamed for abandoning the push for safety: if buyers weren't interested in safety features, like seat belts, why should carmakers care? It is a point worth debating: does any manufacturer have a duty to make a product as safe as possible, regardless of whether or not customers are interested?

In any case, it was left to governments, as it often is, to improve car safety. By the 1960s increased car fatalities alarmed officials. In

AN EARLY CRASH TEST DUMMY SEATED IN A FORD THUNDERBIRD. THE DUMMIES HELPED ENGINEERS UNDER-STAND HOW PEOPLE BECAME INJURED IN A CRASH. THE DISCOVERY THAT THE GREATEST DAMAGE WAS CAUSED WHEN PEOPLE WERE THROWN FROM THE CAR LED TO THE USE OF SEAT BELTS.

IN TIME, IT WAS LEARNED THAT THE SAFEST SEAT BELTS ENCLOSED BOTH THE CHEST AND WAIST, AS SHOWN HERE.

1962 Wisconsin required that all new cars sold in the state have seat belts. Twenty-two other states soon followed Wisconsin's example, and the car industry was forced to make seat belts standard equipment on new vehicles.

The national government, too, began to press carmakers on safety. In 1967 a steering column that collapsed in a crash was introduced, which eventually became standard. In 1972 Ford put airbags in some of its cars, although the safety of airbags themselves remains controversial. In 1977 Tennessee passed a law requiring seat restraints for children. Results were good, and other states followed Tennessee's example. In 1984 New York State made the use of seat belts mandatory: drivers could be fined if they did not buckle up.

In a way the most revolutionary—and least obeyed—safety law was what was initially the national 55 miles (88.6 kilometers) per hour speed limit. Even though it was more frequently ignored than not, it reduced automobile deaths by 20 percent. It was, however, highly unpopular and impossible to enforce. The fact remains that Americans today are driving faster than ever. Only a few years ago people rarely drove more than 65 miles (104.7 kilometers) per hour even on six-lane highways; today driving at 75 miles (120.8 kilometers) or more per hour is routine. A big part of the safety problem lies in the attitude of many Americans, who see speed limits, laws against cell phones, DWI laws, and seat-belt requirements as interfering with their freedom. They do not always realize that reckless driving endangers not only themselves, but others as well. Unfortunately, many lawmakers are reluctant to annoy voters by introducing tougher safety laws. The attitude of the automobile industry is similar. It would be simple technically to put devices in cars limiting their speed and to put entertainment and audio systems in backseats where drivers could not fiddle with them without pulling over, for example. Fatalities could be reduced by suspending the licenses of drivers, especially young drivers, for long periods for breaking speed limits or driving and drinking. Drivers who knew that they would lose their licenses for six months for speeding, or five years for a third conviction, would learn to be more careful. Laws like these in Europe have substantially reduced drunken driving; many Europeans are careful not to drink at all if they know they have to drive. (It must be said, however, that many Europeans drive at speeds most Americans would find hair raising. Automobile fatalities in France have risen so much that the French government is now introducing very tough speeding laws.) A concerted effort by government officials, the auto industry, and drivers could create much safer roads in America; but so far the effort has been halfhearted.

WHILE AMERICANS OFTEN DRIVE FAST, MANY EUROPEANS DRIVE EVEN FASTER. IN SOME PARTS OF EUROPE, THERE ARE NO SPEED LIMITS. INEVITABLY, THE DEATH RATE FROM AUTO ACCIDENTS IS HIGH. HERE, A PHOTOGRAPH CAPTURES THE AFTERMATH OF A MULTICAR ACCIDENT NEAR PARIS, FRANCE.

A second grave problem associated with automobiles is the question of air pollution and

SMOG, PRODUCED FROM SEVERAL SOURCES, INCLUDING AUTOMOBILE EXHAUST, CAN CAUSE A VARIETY OF DIFFERENT ILLNESSES. HERE, A VOLUNTEER OFFERS FRESH AIR TO A LOS ANGELES WOMAN AFFECTED BY SEVERAL DAYS OF LINGERING POLLUTION.

global warming. This is a controversial subject: carmakers and leaders of "smokestack" industries continue to insist that global warming has not been proven, is not a serious danger, or even doesn't exist at all. Some even claim that recent rises in temperature are due to the normal fluctuations we have seen throughout history.

However, by far the majority of scientists believe that global warming has been shown to exist beyond a reasonable doubt, and that its effects can, and eventually will, be catastrophic. The U.S. government now agrees. If it continues, temperate lands like the United States, where a huge portion of the world's food is grown, may become too hot for crops like wheat and corn. For another, the melting of the polar ice caps will dump billions of gallons of water into the seas, raising their levels so that seaport cities like New York, Los Angeles, New Orleans, London, and Venice will flood. Global warming will have other, if more subtle, effects.

But even if we discount global warming altogether, it is indisputable that automobile exhaust causes health problems for millions of Americans. This in turn costs the country billions of dollars in medical expenses every year. Various types of cancer are linked to auto pollutants. Respiratory problems like asthma and emphysema are aggravated by auto exhaust, and people with severe cases of these diseases may die when pollution levels are high. Even for the healthy, the smog produced by air pollution stings people's eyes and makes life generally uncomfortable. There are many very good reasons for trying to curb auto pollution. Unfortunately, as in the case of reckless driving, neither governments nor automobile manufacturers have done as much as they could to eliminate it.

When the car first appeared in American streets, it was believed that it would produce cleaner cities. The health dangers posed by the huge amounts of poisonous gases that cars spewed into the air were never fully considered or understood.

Then, in the early 1950s, a scientist named A. J. Haagen-Smit saw the connection between hydrocarbons and oxides of nitrogen in car exhaust and smog. In 1959 the city of Los Angeles began to regulate pollutants to reduce eye irritants. In 1971 the state of California passed clean-air rules, and in 1974 the federal government started to phase out leaded gasoline. Today the federal government requires cars to use pollution-control systems, but far more could be done.

Global warming and air pollution are not caused by cars alone. Many industries emit tons of pollutants into the air every day. Dry-cleaning fluids, aerosol sprays, and many other products also contribute. But the automobile remains a large source of pollutants.

Unfortunately, over the past half century since we have known that exhaust gases cause medical and other problems, the automobile industry has fought relentlessly against government attempts to control pollutants. Every time a city, state, or federal agency tries to pass laws regulating automobile pollutants, safety, and other matters, the carmakers have sent dozens of highly paid lobbyists to argue against such controls. The industry also gives generously to the election campaigns of state legislators, members of Congress, governors, and presidents, in the hope of influencing them. A government official who sides with the automobile industry is likely to receive large campaign contributions from Ford, General Motors, and the rest. Conversely, legislators who urge tough safety and pollution controls are liable to find themselves facing well-financed opponents in the next election.

Carmakers are not alone in making these sorts of campaign contributions to legislators they favor; all large industries do it. But carmakers are among the leaders. The simple truth is that most of the biggest corporations in the industrial world are automobile and oil companies. They have tremendous wealth and great power. If they had been actively working to control emissions over the past few decades, global warming and air pollution would have been drastically curtailed by now. Instead they have fought hard against controlling these problems.

Questions of pollution and auto safety lead us to another issue that has troubled many: are Americans too much in thrall to the automo-

LOS ANGELES IS ONE OF THE GREAT EXAMPLES OF A CITY WHERE DEPENDENCE ON AUTOMOBILES, RATHER THAN ON MASS TRANSPORTATION, HAS LED TO ENDLESS PROBLEMS AND GREAT EXPENSE. THE PEOPLE DRIVING IN THEIR CARS ON THESE CROWDED HIGHWAYS COULD HAVE BEEN TRANSPORTED MORE CHEAPLY AND EFFICIENTLY BY TRAINS AND BUSES, AS CITY RESIDENTS AND OFFICIALS ARE NOW DISCOVERING.

bile? To put it simply, are we driving our cars too much? The idea of putting limits on how much people may drive their cars in the course of a year—for example, 10,000 miles (16,100 kilometers) annually—may seem absurd; after all, many Americans drive 100 miles (161 kilometers) or more to and from work every day. And yet it is clear enough that we could greatly reduce pollution, automobile fatalities, and the waste of resources that could be better used on other things—such as medicine and housing—if we got out of our cars and into subways, buses, and trains.

The automobile culture that exists in the United States and elsewhere in the industrial world did not come about entirely by chance. Classic cases are the stories of what happened in two great cities, Los Angeles and New York. In 1935 the city of Los Angeles had a very good mass-transportation system built around electric trains and trolleys. In 1938 General Motors, Firestone, and Standard Oil teamed up to destroy that system. They organized Pacific City Lines with the aim of motorizing the electric mass-transit system. They bought the system, scrapped the trains, pulled down the power lines, and tore up the tracks. They then introduced a bus system. The goal, said one investigator for the U.S. government, was to "convert electronic transit systems in sixteen states to General Motors' bus operations."

In the end, state and local governments had to build the mammoth complex of highways, bridges, and superhighways that crisscross Los Angeles. By the 1960s, smog was making the city unpleasant to live in. Today Los Angeles is desperately trying to rebuild the mass-transit system that was so wantonly scrapped. Such an ambitious project, though, will cost huge amounts of money and will be years in the making.

In New York the effort to "automobilize" the city was not led by carmakers, but by a brilliant, power-hungry city planner named Robert Moses. He built many parks and housing projects, but was mainly known for constructing the huge system of highways and bridges that cut through and around New York City and neighboring Long Island. From the 1920s on he ruthlessly destroyed poorer neighborhoods, forc-

THE POWERFUL ROBERT MOSES IS SHOWN HERE WITH A MODEL OF A BRIDGE HE HOPED THE CITY OF NEW YORK WOULD BUILD ACROSS ITS HARBOR. IT WAS NEVER BUILT, BUT SEVERAL OTHERS WERE UNDER HIS TUTELAGE. MOSES WAS DETERMINED TO MAKE NEW YORK AN AUTOMOBILE-FRIENDLY AREA AT THE EXPENSE OF MASS TRANSPORTATION. THE METROPOLITAN AREA NOW SUFFERS FROM CHRONIC TRAFFIC JAMS, LACK OF AVAILABLE PARKING, AND MANY OTHER PROBLEMS BROUGHT ABOUT BY THE OVERUSE OF AUTOMOBILES.

ing the people living there to resettle elsewhere. By the 1960s people were becoming enraged by his high-handed attempts to build roads and parking lots in city parks and squares, and he was forced from power. But in his four decades in various offices he had turned New York into a city for automobiles.

Even at the time many people felt that the money poured into highways and bridges would have been better spent on bolstering the mass-transit system—improving the subways and increasing bus and train service. They were right. What happened was what always happens. If you widen highways and build new bridges and tunnels, for a brief period traffic flows more easily and there are fewer traffic jams. But the

RIDING ON A TRAIN OR A BUS CAN BE FAR MORE RELAXING THAN WRANGLING WITH HEAVY TRAFFIC. IT IS ALSO CHEAPER AND CREATES LESS POLLUTION. NONETHELESS, AMERICANS CONTINUE TO DRIVE THEIR CARS TO WORK EVEN IN AREAS WHERE EXTENSIVE MASS-TRANSPORTATION NETWORKS ARE AVAILABLE.

new ease of driving only encourages people to use their cars all the more. Additional cars crowd onto the highways, and the system is once again glutted. Despite Moses's huge road-building program, traffic problems in New York City are far worse than when Moses began his road program.

It is perfectly clear to everyone who has seriously thought about it that Americans ought to be leaving their cars at home more frequently and taking trains, subways, and buses instead. This is particularly true of people who must commute to work, the majority of American workers.

A subway or train carrying hundreds of people to work is far more economical to run than a car carrying one person along a highway. Air pollution would be greatly reduced, as would the number of highway-related deaths. The resources now going into making cars, building roads, refining gas, and importing oil could be used for other things. The benefits of a large-scale movement from the car to mass transit would be huge.

Mayors of most of America's big cities are well aware of what automobiles cost their cities—and in the end, the taxpayers. The upkeep and repair of streets, bridges, and tunnels; the salaries of traffic-enforcement officers; the maintenance of traffic lights and signs; the damage and delay caused by accidents; the medical costs of pollution—all of these run to billions of dollars annually. Mayors have tried many tactics to move people out of cars and onto subways and buses. They have built new mass-transit systems and upgraded old ones. They have increased bridge, tunnel, and highway tolls—in New York City some tolls are $4 each way, costing regular commuters $40 per week. They have passed laws forbidding cars containing only one person from entering their cities during rush hours or using specific faster highway lanes. They have also raised parking fees and the fines for violations.

Nothing seems to discourage drivers. They seem to be willing to pay almost any price to drive their cars. No matter how much we blame the automobile industry for encouraging the car culture, or the government for failing to control it, the real culprit is the American driver. The simple truth is that Americans like to drive their cars. Millions of them would rather drive to work, to baseball games and concerts, to classes, or to anywhere else than take mass transit. There are, of course, advantages to driving: the driver is not tied to a train schedule, does not have to walk to a bus stop in the rain, and is more comfortable than on a crowded subway.

But the costs, direct and indirect, far outweigh the convenience. To most, it doesn't matter: driving gives people a sense of freedom, of being in control of their lives. It gives them a feeling of power and even importance.

THIS EXPERIMENTAL CAR HAS BEEN DESIGNED BY TOYOTA FOR CHINA, WHERE IMMENSE TRAFFIC JAMS AND HIGH LEVELS OF AIR POLLUTION EXIST IN CITIES LIKE BEIJING AND SHANGHAI.

There is a pride in car ownership that doesn't come with a temporary seat on a subway or train.

So, until Americans are persuaded that it is not in their best interests to drive, America will continue to be a car-centered culture. Americans are not alone. Throughout the world, whenever a nation begins to industrialize and grow in prosperity, traffic jams and air pollution are sure to follow. Only a generation ago in cities like Beijing in China, Bangkok in Thailand, and Jakarta in Indonesia, only the wealthy owned cars. Today the streets of these cities are packed with traffic, although fortunately the Chinese government has been quick to notice the problem and is requiring its carmakers to build vehicles that get good gas mileage and have some pollution controls.

Cars have brought great blessings to humankind, but they have brought problems as well. It will take much thought and effort before human beings learn to use their automobiles wisely.

automatic transmission—A system in which gear ratios are changed automatically and not manually by the driver.

axle—One of typically two crossbeams or shafts that support the weight of the vehicle and on which wheels rotate.

benzene engine—An early motor that ran on a hydrocarbon-based fuel.

carburetor—A device that mixes fuel and air in a certain proportion to allow for proper combustion.

cylinder—A circular hole inside an engine block that provides space for a piston to move.

differential—A system of gears located midway between two wheels, allowing them to spin at different speeds when the vehicle corners.

drivetrain—A combination of parts that connects the transmission with the vehicle's driving axles. In general, all the moving parts of a car including the engine, clutch, transmission, driveshaft, differential, axles, and wheels.

engine block—The main part of the motor, where the pistons and valves are located and move.

flywheel—A heavy disk attached to the rear end of the crankshaft, which when turned rotates the crankshaft and gives the engine its initial starting motion.

four-stroke cycle—An internal-combustion engine that requires two revolutions per cylinder amounting to four piston strokes. The cycle is comprised of a power stroke, a compression stroke, another power stroke, then an exhaust stroke.

horsepower—A unit of measure for quantifying the output of power. Originally equal to the amount of effort a horse expended in raising 33,000 pounds 1 foot in one minute.

"hot tube"—A device used for igniting fuel, in which a narrow tube is heated from outside the combustion chamber of the cylinder by an intense flame.

H-plan gearshift—A pattern of shift positions, for a manual transmission, arranged in the shape of an H.

hydraulic—Relating to the process in which fluid is forced along one end of a tube or pipe, exerting pressure on the other end.

interchangeability of parts—The quality of individual items making up a manufactured product being of uniform shape and size so they can be assembled into any similar product.

internal-combustion engine—An engine in which the fuel is consumed on the inside, where heat expands a gas to either move a piston or turn a turbine.

mass production—Manufacturing an item on a large scale, a process dependent on all the same parts being made exactly alike.

piston—A partly hollow, cylinder-shaped metal part that is connected to the crankshaft via a connecting rod, closed at one end, and fitted with rings to seal it as it moves within the engine cylinder.

pneumatic—Referring to the power achieved when air is placed within a sealed tube as in a tire; or as used to boost the operating force of power brakes.

two-stroke stationary engine—An internal-combustion engine that requires only two piston strokes or one complete up-and-down revolution per cylinder to achieve power.

1712
Englishman Thomas Newcomen builds the first practical steam engine.

1862
French researcher Alphonse-Eugène Beau de Rochas first presents his theory of the four-stroke cycle engine.

1876
German inventor Nikolaus Otto builds the first practical four-stroke piston cycle internal-combustion engine.

1885
Gottlieb Daimler and Wilhelm Maybach patent their design for the four-stroke engine.

1886
Carl Benz registers his patent for a three-wheeled vehicle with a four-stroke engine.

1891
French engineers named Émile Levassor and René Panhard produce the prototype for the modern automobile.

1899
Approximately thirty U.S. auto manufacturers produce an estimated 2,500 cars. There are about 8,000 total automobiles in existence in the United States.

1900
Steering wheels begin to replace tillers.
One out of every 9,500 Americans owns an automobile—40 percent steam powered, 38 percent electric, and 22 percent had gasoline-powered internal-combustion engines.

1901
Oldsmobile offers its first model equipped with a speedometer.
License plates first appear on U.S. models.

1903
The Ford Motor Company is organized.

1904
William "Billy" Durant joins the nearly bankrupt Buick Motor Car Company.

1907
A Paris newspaper sponsors the first long-distance auto race. Five entrants leave Beijing, China, on June 10. The winner arrives in Paris on August 10.

1908
The first Model Ts are offered for sale.
With the acquisition of Buick, Oldsmobile, Cadillac, and Oakland (which would become Pontiac), General Motors is formed.

1910
The first production vehicle to contain a V8 is built by De Dion Bouton in France.

1911
Forced out of General Motors, Billy Durant joins Louis Chevrolet to establish Chevrolet Motor Car Company.

1913
Henry Ford installs the first moving assembly line, which is able to produce up to 1,000 cars per day.

1914
Forty-eight percent of all cars on American roads are Model Ts.

1918
The first three-color stop light is installed, in Detroit.
Chevrolet is acquired by General Motors.

1923
For the first time, sales of closed cars surpass those of open cars.
More than half the cars purchased in the United States are bought on a credit plan.

1926
Power steering is developed but is not fully integrated into production models until 1951.
Benz and Daimler merge.

1927
Ford's Model T is discontinued, replaced by the Model A.

1929
U.S. car production reaches more than 5.3 million, a mark not surpassed until 1949.

1931
The United States has 830,000 miles of paved highways.

1935
Parking meters are first installed in Oklahoma City, Oklahoma.
The United Automobile Workers (UAW) union is formed.

1937
The gearshift is first moved from the floor to the steering column.

1940
General Motors introduces the automatic transmission.

1941
Taking his initial inspiration from fighter planes, starting in this year, Harley Earl revolutionizes car design.

1942
Standard auto production halts during World War II. Gas rationing begins.

1945
The first Volkswagen Beetle is produced.

1947
Henry Ford dies at the age of eighty-three.

1949
Chrysler introduces the first model started exclusively by turning the key in the ignition.

1951
Chrysler releases its first cars with power steering.

1954
Manufacturers Studebaker and Packard merge their operations.

1957
The first Edsels come off Ford's production lines.

1958
Cruise control becomes available.

1964
Studebaker-Packard becomes the first U.S. manufacturer to offer front seat belts as a standard feature.
The Ford Mustang is released.

1974
General Motors introduces the catalytic converter to comply with provisions in the Federal Clean Air Act.

1980
Japan emerges as the world's leading auto manufacturer, with more than 11 million vehicles produced. The United States had held that distinction for seventy-six years.

1981
The United Auto Workers (UAW) enters into talks with major U.S. manufacturers as recession deepens and imported models continue to flood the American market.

1987
The Ford Motor Company earns record profits, $4.6 billion.

1988

Chrysler becomes the first to offer air bag restraint systems as standard equipment.

1991

The Ford Motor Company posts its largest one-year loss, $2.3 billion.

1992

Reflecting the ongoing trend to larger vehicles, the Hummer, or high-mobility multipurpose wheeled vehicle, a military model, enters the mainstream, civilian market.

2001

Pontiac celebrates seventy-five years of operation.

Web Sites

http://inventors.about.com/library/inventors/blcar.htm
http://inventors.about.com/library/weekly/aacarsgasa.htm
A multipart overview of automobile history.

http://www.autoshop-online.com/auto101/histtext.html
A commercial site, but the link will connect you with an extensive
and informative page on the development and social impact of the automobile.

http://www.si.edu/resource/faq/nmah/autohist.htm
Sponsored by the Smithsonian Institution, this page offers an extensive bibliography of print resources on car-related subjects.

http://members.tripod.com/~Eagle_Planet/carshistory.html
A two-part examination of automobile history.

http://www.themuseumofautomobilehistory.com/
The official site of the Museum of Automobile History. Go to the
museum in person or make a virtual visit.

There have been thousands of books published on automobiles, and hundreds are available in libraries and bookstores today. There are volumes on every make of car, major and minor. For general automotive history, the following heavily illustrated books may be useful:

Adler, Dennis. *The Art of the Automobile: The 100 Greatest Cars.* New York: HarperCollins, 2000.
A recent and helpful overview.

Drehsen, Wolf, and Halwart Schrader, eds. *The Schlumpf Automobile Collection.* West Chester, PA: Schiffer, 1989.
This title includes coverage of antique and veteran cars.

Stein, Ralph. *The Greatest Cars.* New York: Simon & Schuster, 1979.
An older title, but it is often found in libraries and offers an informative guide to the general history of cars.

Index

Page numbers for illustrations are in **boldface**.

About the Author

James Lincoln Collier has written books for both adults and students on many subjects, among them the prizewinning novel *My Brother Sam Is Dead.* Many of these books, both fiction and nonfiction, have historical themes, including the highly acclaimed Marshall Cavendish Benchmark series the Drama of American History, which he wrote with Christopher Collier.